How to Increase Sales through Discounted Coupon Codes

The Success and Pitfalls of Coupon Codes

By: Anne Marie Collins

9781681279473

PUBLISHERS NOTES

Disclaimer – Speedy Publishing LLC

This publication is intended to provide helpful and informative material. It is not intended to diagnose, treat, cure, or prevent any health problem or condition, nor is intended to replace the advice of a physician. No action should be taken solely on the contents of this book. Always consult your physician or qualified health-care professional on any matters regarding your health and before adopting any suggestions in this book or drawing inferences from it.

The author and publisher specifically disclaim all responsibility for any liability, loss or risk, personal or otherwise, which is incurred as a consequence, directly or indirectly, from the use or application of any contents of this book.

Any and all product names referenced within this book are the trademarks of their respective owners. None of these owners have sponsored, authorized, endorsed, or approved this book.

Always read all information provided by the manufacturers' product labels before using their products. The author and publisher are not responsible for claims made by manufacturers.

This book was originally printed before 2014. This is an adapted reprint by Speedy Publishing LLC with newly updated content designed to help readers with much more accurate and timely information and data.

Speedy Publishing LLC

40 E Main Street, Newark, Delaware, 19711

Contact Us: 1-888-248-4521

Website: http://www.speedypublishing.co

REPRINTED Paperback Edition: 9781681279473:

Manufactured in the United States of America

Dedication

This book is dedicated to my mother, the Mistress of Coupon Codes, Janet. Yes, you are frugal but that frugality helped our family greatly especially in times of great distress. Thanks, Mom!

TABLE OF CONTENTS

Chapter 1- The Usual and Not-so-Usual Reasons for Shopping Online 5

Chapter 2- A Step-by-Step Guide to Online Shopping 11

Chapter 3- How Does a Coupon Code Work? 15

Chapter 4- Familiarizing the Different Kinds of Coupon Codes . 19

Chapter 5- How do Businesses Use Coupon Codes in their Marketing Strategy? 23

Chapter 6 - How to Create Coupons? 28

Chapter 7- How Much Savings Are Expected With Coupon Codes? 32

Chapter 8- Reasons for Using Coupon Codes 38

Chapter 9- Maximizing Coupon Codes 43

Chapter 10- Where Can Your Customers Find Your Coupons? .. 49

About The Author 64

CHAPTER 1- THE USUAL AND NOT-SO-USUAL REASONS FOR SHOPPING ONLINE

Online shopping is a phenomenon that has changed the way we shop for the things we use and need in our day to day lives. An informal survey of web users who frequent an Internet bulletin board that is geared to online shopping reveals that over 90 percent buy products and services online at least once a month, and many of these people make it a habit to shop online several times a week. What is it about this practice that makes them keep going back for more?

If you are one of those people who have yet to shop online, or if you have perhaps completed only one or two transactions online, you don't know what you are missing! Not only have you not experienced the fun of hunting down a good online deal, but you haven't had the satisfaction of saving a bundle of cash on the things you would be buying anyway, online or in a brick and mortar

How to Increase Sales through Discounted Coupon Codes

store. Everything that you buy offline can more than likely be found online – from groceries to prescription drugs.

"Sure," you may be thinking. "Online shopping is probably a good thing for people who live miles away from a store. It would almost be a necessity for them in order to have a good selection. But I have all sorts of stores really close to my home. It's more convenient for me to shop the way I always have."

That depends entirely on how you define convenience. Is this really easy?

- You get into your car and drive to the store of your choice, then drive around the parking lot a few times looking for a parking space.

- Entering the store, you walk the aisles looking for the things on your list, only to find that they are out of the two most important things you need.

- You go back out to your car and drive to your second choice store.

- Finally locating the items you need, you stand in an extremely long check-out line behind a woman with a set of 2 year old twins who are screaming for candy.

- The cashier is cranky, and acts as if she would rather be doing anything other than her job.

- You start back out to your car with your packages, and discover that it is pouring rain. You have no umbrella, and your car is parked way in the back of the lot – the only empty space you could find.

Anne Marie Collins

- You brave the elements, and make a run for your car, only dropping your packages once. Dripping wet, you turn on the ignition and head for home. It's late afternoon, and the traffic is horrendous. As you inch along, you hear a suspicious little taptaptap on your windshield. A closer look and you groan aloud. The rain has turned into ice.

Meanwhile, your next door neighbor has decided that she is in need of a few health and beauty products. She sits down at her computer in the comfort of her nice, cozy den. A few clicks of her mouse, and her web browser has taken her to an online drugstore that actually offers more of a product variety than the local drugstore that is only a mile from her house. She smiles when she discovers that several of the items on her list are on sale.

As she reaches the screen where she is to finalize her order, she remembers an email she received from this website yesterday. It contained a coupon code that will give her free shipping when she purchases a certain dollar amount. Scanning her order, she sees that she needs to spend $1 more to take advantage of this code. Another few clicks and she has added a toothbrush to her virtual shopping cart.

As she clicks the "Place Order Now" icon button, she smiles. That one little code has saved her $8.00! Hearing a sound from outside, she rises and steps over to the window. Pulling back the curtain, she looks outside. It has begun to sleet!

She smiles again as she thinks how nice it is not to have to brave the cold and instead, be able to shop from home and have the order delivered right to her front door.

How to Increase Sales through Discounted Coupon Codes

Which scenario would you rather find yourself in? The answer should be obvious. Internet shopping can be a much easier alternative for you, especially if you –

- Work long or odd hours and have trouble finding the time to shop after work

- Lack reliable transportation

- Have small children that are difficult to handle on a shopping trip

- Have any sort of physical disability which limits your mobility

- Are looking for items not readily available in your area, such as ethnic foods, classic fragrances, or large shoe and clothing sizes.

Save More Time than You Can Imagine

Shopping online can save you more time than you could imagine. As is illustrated in the scenario above, it is much less of a hassle to make purchases from home, from your office, or anywhere you happen to find a computer than it is to physically shop at the mall or the grocery store. Plus, if you want to shop at 2 AM while wearing your pajamas, you can do that, too!

Online shopping is a lifesaver for Christmas shopping. While everyone else is fighting the crowds, you are greeting the UPS or FedEx driver as your boxes are delivered. You can easily purchase items for gifts without others knowing what you're buying, which comes in very handy when you need to buy gifts for people who live in your home with you. Or maybe you are in need of something that you would rather not have other people know that you use. Online shopping can save you the embarrassment of having nosy strangers or even family members observe your buying habits.

Anne Marie Collins

Comparison shopping is a breeze on the Internet. Instead of having to make phone call after phone call, or walk/drive from store to store in search of a product you need, you can do a search on Google or another search engine in order to locate the best price for an item. Once you locate what you're looking for at a price you want to pay, you are ready to order!

Now, imagine how much more difficult this would have been if you were doing it all the old fashioned way. Let's say you had to visit 10 web sites in order to find the exact product you wanted at a reasonable price. Transpose this shopping equation to real life. By the time you got done with searching 10 brick and mortar stores, you'd be exhausted, and you might even cut your search short and buy the product at a higher price than you had expected to pay in order to finish your shopping and go home! With online shopping, you won't have this problem.

"But I need an item TODAY," you might say. "I don't want to have to wait until an online store can ship my purchase to me!" If you are in a hurry for an item, you can sometimes order it online and then pick it up at the store, as long as there is a store available in your area. Office supply stores and department stores with a web presence usually offer this feature to their online customers. It can be a real time saver as all you need to do is go to the Customer Service desk to pick up your order.

You can also choose to pay an extra shipping fee when ordering online in order to have your items sent to you sooner, even overnight, but the cost of this could very well negate any savings you may have realized by using a coupon code.

Here is where you have to sit down and decide what your priorities are. Is the hassle of navigating your way through crowded stores and having to search for the items you want to buy, plus the chore

How to Increase Sales through Discounted Coupon Codes
of standing in long checkout lines to pay for the items better than the convenience of ordering the items online and having to wait a few days before you receive your order?

For most people, the convenience of online shopping far outweighs the minor inconvenience of not being able to take possession of their purchase immediately. Try both scenarios, and then make your decision. I'll bet you choose online shopping!

This is probably why online shopping has become one of the most popular ways to shop. You have so many choices, and can custom tailor your shopping habits to suit yourself.

Chapter 2 - A Step-by-Step Guide to Online Shopping

Let's walk through the steps that a shopper takes when they want to purchase a product online. Of course, online shopping is exactly what the term implies, but for anyone who is not familiar with exactly what to do, the following information should be helpful.

- Decide what you are looking for. Yes, they sell almost anything you can imagine online, so the chances are good that you will be able to find exactly what you need.

- Using a good search engine like Google, find several web sites that sell the item you want. Don't just stop at the first site you come across. You want to find both the best quality and also the best price you can.

How to Increase Sales through Discounted Coupon Codes

- If you are unsure as to the brand name or style you are seeking, you can also Google product reviews for the item you are seeking to get recommendations from others.

- You may also want to take the time to browse one of several product comparison sites that are available on the web to help shoppers in their quest to find just what they are looking for.

- Once you have settled upon a web site that sells the product you are looking for, browse the site until you decide which size, color or variety you want.

- Look for an icon button that says "Add to Cart" or a similar phrase.

- Choose how many you want of the item. If there are any other choices such as size or color, this is the point where you select them.

- Your items will be added to your virtual online cart. There should also be an icon button that you can use to edit your shopping cart if you have made a mistake.

- If you want to continue shopping, there will be an icon button to click that says "Continue Shopping" or something similar, and it will take you back to the section of the web site where you can select another item.

- If you are done shopping, look for an icon button that says "Checkout" or something similar. This will take you to another page where you will fill out a form with your name and the address where you want the item sent. You'll also need to input your email address and telephone number.

- Are you are sending this item to someone as a gift? You will need to look for a box to check that specifies this. Look for "Is This Item a Gift?" or something similar. Check it off, and if you like, select a gift wrap option either for free or for a small fee.

- There will be a space for your credit card information. Many people get very nervous about entering their credit card info on a web site. This is a needless worry, for all reputable merchant web sites are designed to be secure.

- Look down at the bottom of your browser. Do you see a small icon that looks like a padlock? If it is in the locked position, your info is quite safe. If the icon shows an open lock, you might want to think twice about placing your card number on this site. You should call this to the attention of the webmaster for the web site.

- Not only will you enter your card number and expiration date, but also the 3 or 4 digit code from the back of your credit card. This is an attempt by online merchants to control credit card fraud. By requiring this code, no one can get your card number off of your restaurant check or credit card receipt and fraudulently use it online to purchase goods and services.

- Usually, there is a space on the form for a coupon or gift card code. This will be explained in more detail later in this report.

- Once you have filled in all of this information, your web browser will go to the next page. This will be your order confirmation page. Look over this page carefully, perhaps double checking your credit card number for accuracy. Then, confirm your order by clicking the button icon that says "Place Your Order" or something similar.

How to Increase Sales through Discounted Coupon Codes
- You'll now see a page thanking you for your order. There will be an order confirmation number among the information given here, so it's a good idea to print this entire page for your records. You should also get an email copy of this page.

- Sit back, relax, and wait for your order to arrive! You should receive an email when your package ships that contains a tracking number. You can track the whereabouts of your package and also find out when it is scheduled for delivery by going to the UPS or FedEx web site.

Chapter 3 - How Does a Coupon Code Work?

Remember our online shopper at the beginning of this report? When she got to the web page to finalize her order, she remembered a coupon code that would give her free shipping on her order. Online retailers provide these codes to their customers as a form of advertising. They know that a good coupon code will bring the following three types of traffic to their site.

- New customer traffic – consumers who may not have ever shopped with them before.

- Previous customer traffic - consumers that came back to shop again because of the coupon code discount.

How to Increase Sales through Discounted Coupon Codes

- Repeat business traffic – consumers who are so pleased with the items they purchased at a discount that they come back to purchase other items, possibly at full price. This is considered the best type of traffic.

Coupon codes are a win-win promotion both for the shopper and the retailer who offers them. You get a good deal, and the retailer gets an increase in traffic. Unlike coupons that you cut out of the newspaper or magazines, online coupon codes can't be lost or replaced. You can use the code once, and then pass it along to a friend or family member so that they can get a good online deal, too. Many a convert to online shopping has been made with the sharing of just one good coupon code!

Be aware that some coupon codes expire very quickly, while others can be valid for quite some time. When you enter the code, whatever discount it represents is immediately taken off of the total of your order. It's a good idea to check your total on the checkout page once you refresh it to make sure the code went through.

Occasionally, coupon codes are removed without notice by the retailer. And, sometimes a coupon code is so popular that the web site where you use it is jammed with customers! If this happens, you might have to try your code more than one time to get it to go through. If you've done this, and your coupon code still does not work, a call to the Customer Service department of the retailer might be in order. Usually, the telephone number to call if you have any questions is listed somewhere on the web site.

Some web sites also have live help where you can actually chat with a customer representative in an instant-message type setting. They are quick to answer any questions you might have, as they realize that a happy customer is usually a repeat customer. Or, look for the store's email address. This is just one of the many neat things about shopping on the Internet — most of the time, help is but a mouse click away.

Make sure you understand the terms of the coupon code. If it states that you must spend $25 to get that 10% off, don't think you can squeak by with spending $24.98! You have to spend the stated amount down to the last cent. Luckily, most online stores will have items for sale that are quite cheap — in the case of Amazon.com. 5 cents or even less! This makes it easy to add another item to your shopping cart to bring up your total.

Also, don't confuse coupon codes with rebates! Unlike a manufacturer's mail in rebate, an online coupon code saves you money the instant you use it.

How Coupon Codes are Used in a Business

Now, I want you to take out a sheet of paper or open up your word processor and think of the products or services in your business that you could offer a discount on.

Here's what my list looks like:

I could:

1. Offer a discount on my consulting services.

2. Offer a buy one get one free offer on advertising services I offer.

3. Offer a coupon for free stuff when someone joins one of my membership sites.

4. Offer a $X discount on my eBooks, and software.

How to Increase Sales through Discounted Coupon Codes

I know your business may be different than mine, but you can still find at least one thing to offer a discount on or a free offer for buying what you are selling. If you can't think of anything, compile a list of everything your business offers, then go back over that list, and I am sure you will find something. If you STILL can't find something, then my advice would be to develop or buy something inexpensive that you can either give away free or offer a discount on to achieve the goal you have for using coupons.

Chapter 4- Familiarizing the Different Kinds of Coupon Codes

Coupon codes are called promotional codes by some online retailers. Don't let this confuse you – they are the same thing, really. Most of the time, the online codes are a series of numbers, numbers and letters mixed, or a short word that relates to the type of retailer, usually in all capital letters. For example, a PetSmart code could look like this –

- MEOW838

Another type of code is a clickable link that leads you to a page where a number/letter code will be displayed for you to enter when you check out. These codes are often included in email newsletters that online retailers send to customers who have signed up for them.

If you think about it, you'll realize that an online coupon is merely a more modern version of the coupons shoppers have been clipping from the Sunday newspaper inserts for many years. And, like those

How to Increase Sales through Discounted Coupon Codes
paper coupons, online coupons can be found for almost any product that is sold on the Internet. You should be able to find coupon codes for the following -

- Clothing for Men, Women and Children

- Auto accessories

- Health and Beauty Ads

- Pet Food and Accessories

- Magazines and Books

- Computers and computer accessories

- Gifts and Flowers

- Electronics

- Furniture

- Food

- Sporting Goods

- Shoes

- Jewelry

- Art and Photography

- Office Supplies

- Online Services

- Music CDs, Movie DVDs, Video Games'

- Kitchen accessories, including cookware

- Gardening and Outdoor supplies

- Toys and Games

- Cigarettes and Cigars

- Airline Tickets

- Concert and Event Tickets

- Rental Cars

- Hotel Accommodations

- Restaurants

In short, anything that is sold on the Internet by a retailer or company, large or small, can have a coupon code associated with it. You will sometimes see multiple codes, and in this case, you should stop and figure out which one would give you the best value. When you are just starting out using coupons online to save money, this all might seem a little confusing. But, after you've completed a transaction or two, you will catch on like an old pro.

For example, let's say that you want to do some shopping at The Body Shop online. Your first step is to visit a website devoted to coupon codes in order to see if there are any current ones for this retailer. You spy not just one, but several codes. There is one that offers you free shipping on your order another which gives you

How to Increase Sales through Discounted Coupon Codes

10% off of the total amount you spend, and another that is for $10 off when you spend $25. How will you know which one to use?

Depending on how much you are planning to spend, it's a tossup between the $10 off and the 10% off. On some web sites, you can use more than one coupon code, which is called stacking. This is a very popular method for maximum savings, and a perfectly legitimate option. You won't know if a retailer will allow the use of multiple codes until you actually type them into the space on the order blank and update the page to see if they went through. If they did, you will notice that your total amount due has been reduced. If they didn't you will see a brief message, sometimes in red text that explains why you were not given the discount. It's well worth your time to try multiple coupon codes each time you shop online!

The codes themselves are somewhat predictable. Generally, they are like the ones in the example above – a percentage or a flat amount off of your total bill, or free shipping. There have also been instances, usually seasonal, where the addition of a special coupon code will yield a free gift.

CHAPTER 5- HOW DO BUSINESSES USE COUPON CODES IN THEIR MARKETING STRATEGY?

The first thing you need to do when deciding on whether or not to use coupons in your marketing strategy is to develop a plan to see if they can work for you.

Here's what your plan outline should look like:

1. How are you going to use the coupons?

- Do you want to use them to generate leads?

- Give a discount on a big-ticket item so you can sell more of that item?

- Get new customers?

How to Increase Sales through Discounted Coupon Codes

- Get customers who haven't purchased from you in a long time to buy from you?

- Other uses?

2. Who is your target market? Who do you want to reach by adding coupons as part of your marketing strategy?

3. What is your budget? Since this strategy can be used for those with a limited budget, you will want to know exactly how much money you have to spend and in what areas are you going to spend it in? Do you want to spend most of your money on presentation or do you want to spend more of your money on the number of people you can reach with your coupons?

4. How are you going to measure your results? You will need some sort of tracking to see how well this strategy works.

The only way coupons will NOT work for you is if you cannot create a plan using the outline above. Using coupons in your marketing is a very powerful strategy, so before throwing the idea out the window use one of your free consulting sessions with me to see if I can help you.

Here's what my last coupon marketing campaign plan looked like. I was offering a coupon for my latest eBook.

1. Coupons will be used to encourage buyers to buy the eBook at a lower price than what it is being offered everywhere else. They will be saving $20. I'll be getting new customers, and probably leads with this coupon campaign.

2. I will be offering this coupon to my customers who have purchased from me in the past to entice them to buy from me

again. I'll also be offering this coupon to my JV partners so they can use it to entice their customers to buy at the low price. This will get me new customers as well.

3. Since I haven't sold any of these, I only have a couple hundred dollars to spend on advertising. I'll be offering these coupons to my JV partners to use so that won't cost me anything, but I'd like to set up a Google AdWords campaign offering the coupon also.

4. I'll be using a special URL for all sales that come through this coupon. I'll be able to track how many sales I get from this coupon via this URL. I'll be able to track the amount of people who visit the site where the coupon is displayed by viewing my logs on my site.

Don't let the above plan scare you. Remember I wrote this plan after using the coupon marketing tactics I am teaching you in this course. Once you are through reading this course you will be able to develop an advanced plan just like the one above.

Examples

I've been in the advertising business for many years and have seen coupons used in thousands of different ways, and in thousands of different businesses. We've all seen the typical X amount of cents off on grocery store coupons. Now even more stores are using coupons that you may be familiar with.

Pharmaceutical stores like Eckerd and Walgreen's now publish an insert in local newspapers that have nothing but coupons for that particular store in them. I know several people who will look for coupons in the paper before doing their shopping for the week. Okay, so you're not a grocery store or big pharmaceutical store, so how can coupons become a powerful marketing tool for you?

How to Increase Sales through Discounted Coupon Codes

Recently I read James Jones' "12 Little-Known, High Profit, Low Startup, Kick Butt Business Ideas for 2005 and Beyond!"

In it he talked about a restaurant he worked at. This restaurant was a small mom and pop type restaurant that did well until a competitor moved in next door. Instead of just going under, this small mom and pop restaurant used the power of coupons to kick their competitors butt. They simply made small buy one lunch get the second lunch free coupons. They distributed these coupons all over their town.

The next day, they were totally swamped with business. After counting all the coupons that had been redeemed for that day, they saw that 22% of the coupons they had given away were used. How many advertising campaigns have you had that gave you a 22% conversion rate? I'd say not many, and probably more like NONE!

Let's talk about some online ways coupons have been used. When I started my web design business in 1998, I had ZERO customers. I had no clue how to get more customers except to offer my services for free and hope for referrals from the people I had done the free web design for.

After doing this a couple of times, I saw that I would never make it if I didn't do something different. I started thinking about how to advertise my business. I knew there was a lot of competition out there for web design services, and I somehow had to stick out. I started by placing classified ads in e-zines.

My ad was offering a 50% discount on all web design services. At that time, web design services where sky high and we were in the age of the "Dot Com Boom". When people started seeing these ads, I was flooded with business. I built sites for these people and also added them to my mailing list.

When business was slow I'd email my list and offer some type of service such as a "website make over service" or tell them about a new technology they could implement on their site, and again give them a discount. Not like the 50% discount they got at first but more like a 20% discount, and this tactic ALWAYS brought in more business.

I've also offered coupons online for other things such as advertising services, consulting services, tangible products, eBooks, software, and the list goes on. Each and every time I offer a coupon I am not disappointed.

People LOVE to save money. How many times have you bought something you really didn't need or want just because it was on sale? As you can see, there are so many ways you can use coupons in your business!

CHAPTER 6 - HOW TO CREATE COUPONS?

In this section I'm going to teach you to make print coupons for your offline promotions, and digital coupons for your online promotions. Let's start with print coupons for your offline promotions.

Now that you know how to create coupons for offline marketing, let's talk about where you can advertise your coupons offline. The most important thing to remember about advertising either online or offline is you need to advertise to your target market. So, when looking for places to advertise your offline coupon, only advertise in places that you target market looks in.

If you are advertising your coupon on car detailing, you don't want to advertise it in the personal ads section of your newspaper, you want to advertise it the Auto section of your paper.

If you are advertising your eBook on how to make money, you don't want to advertise it in a magazine about remodeling. You'd want to find a magazine that was geared towards opportunity seekers, or home based business enthusiasts.

Finding targeted advertising is much easier offline than online in my opinion. It's not instantaneous like online advertising, but I think you can reach your market with it much better. The best places to advertise offline are in print publications.

Putting a coupon in a print publication is one of the best ways to spend your offline advertising dollars. Find a print publication that fits your target market, place your coupon ad in that publication, and I am sure you will be pleased with the results.

Another way I have used print coupons is by mailing them to my mailing list. Let me explain exactly how I do this. Online I have a customer mailing list. When they buy something from me, they supply their mailing address. Instead of emailing them my offer, I simply make the coupons like I did in the video above, print them out and mail the coupons to their home address.

Now I DO NOT suggest that you just send one little coupon out in an envelope. That's a waste of advertising space. You could also make a full-page ad for other things you are offering. Print it out and also include it in the envelope with their coupon. I've been doing this exact same thing since 1998, and believe me if it didn't make me a lot of money, I wouldn't waste my time. Again, these are just a few ways you can offer your coupons offline. I'm sure

How to Increase Sales through Discounted Coupon Codes
you'll get more and more ideas once you start using your coupons offline.

Creating coupons for your online promotions will take a little bit of technical skills, but don't let that scare you. To do the basics (which is all most people need) won't take much at all. In the next section I am going to give you two places you can advertise your coupons online right now for free. I first want to cover some other ways you can advertise your coupons online first.

1. You can place an image of your coupon on your site, and let people know that by purchasing today or for the next X amount of days, they will get a discount. When they click on the coupon, they are taken to your special discount page where they can purchase what you are offering at the special coupon price.

2. Advertise your coupon in your email signature line or signature line you use in forums.

3. Now this is a top secret advertising technique that is getting ready to storm the Internet. Say goodbye to expensive pay-per-click services. You can now advertise in laser targeted information products by going to their website ViralEbooksAds.

This site will allow you to pick your target market from a list that they have. Find a product that matches your target market, place your coupon in that product and you will have unlimited lifetime exposure to your target market. How does it work? Well, you can visit their website, and see, but it's really simple.

Different information products are developed at this site on several different topics. Webmasters and ezine owners give away or sell these products to people who are interested in these topics. Inside the products are ads that are viewed by everyone

Anne Marie Collins

who downloads and uses/reads the products. Therefore the ads inside are being seen by 1000's of different people who are interested in that topic.

4. I know I just got done "bashing" pay per click advertising, but if you are really good at it, you can make a lot of money from using it. I have used pay per click advertising to advertise my coupons, and I've done better advertising them than anything else I have advertised. However, I didn't get the HUGE results I expected. Well, there you go there's several ways you can advertise your coupons online.

5. While compiling this course, a man named Craig Axiaq contacted me. I knew that using coupons was a very powerful technique, but new that I would really open people's eyes with this course. I was so glad when Craig contacted me because he too knew the power of marketing with coupons and had several years of experience with using coupons as a marketing strategy. With the knowledge he has about marketing with coupons, he created his website MyVoucher.

MyVoucher is a one of a kind site that you can join right now. You'll be able to start your own account, and make your own online coupons.

Once you make your coupons, you can advertise the URL of where coupons are located. When people click on your URL they will automatically see your coupon. This site has a ton of other benefits also, and you should check it out. For the first 30 days you can get an account for only $1.

Well, there you go there's several ways you can advertise your coupons online.

Chapter 7 - How Much Savings Are Expected With Coupon Codes?

The popularity of online coupon codes has really begun to catch on, and every day, more and more people are realizing that they can save quite a bit on the things they need when they take advantage of these discounts. With a little planning, you can too!

It helps to have some patience, especially if you are just starting out. Sometimes, you will not be able to find a coupon code for the online store where you want to shop. Though there are usually lots of valid coupon codes circulating around the Web, every store will not always have one listed. If that is the case, you can choose to wait and make your purchase when a code becomes available, or perhaps choose a different store that does have a code that will allow you to save some money.

Another more indirect way that online coupon codes can save you money is the savings you will realize at the gas pump and on your car maintenance. Gasoline prices are high and there seems to be no relief in sight any time soon. When you shop online, you don't have to drive to the store, using up expensive gasoline and putting more miles on your car. On average, depending on the kind of car you drive, it costs anywhere from 35 to 40 cents for each mile you drive – not including the gas! So, it's easy to see how shopping online can help you save a nice chunk of change in a year's time.

We spoke of saving time in the paragraphs above, but the subject is well worth mentioning again. Few people put a price on their time, but you should. Your time is very valuable! Every minute of time that you save by shopping online instead of having to get the car out and drive to the store is a minute that you can put toward making your life more productive. Next time you go to the mall, do a little experiment. Keep track of how much time it takes you to fight the traffic in order to drive there, find the items you are looking for, pay for them, and drive home again. You will be shocked! Now, see how that time can add up over the course of a year? Remember – time is money!

Some people have tried online shopping, and are quite vocal about the cost of shipping. Obviously, they did not pursue the fun of using coupon codes, nor did they even try online shopping more than a time or two. If they had, they would have seen that not only do online coupon codes for free shipping pop up for most retail stores on the web with regularity, but most stores will offer free shipping even without a coupon code if you spend a set amount, usually $30 or so. So, this argument is a moot point. Online shopping with coupon codes can and does save savvy shoppers quite a bit of money!

One thing you need to be aware of is that if you have an actual brick and mortar store in your area that also has an online presence, you will pay sales tax on your purchases from the web. This adds a small amount to your total invoice amount. For example, if you have a Best Buy in your city, and you order an iPod

How to Increase Sales through Discounted Coupon Codes

from BestBuy.com, you'll be charged sales tax. Or, if you purchase a pair of jeans from Old Navy.com, and there is no Old Navy store in your city, you will not have to pay sales tax.

Real Stories from Real People

In the interest of research, I decided to do some online shopping with coupon codes just to demonstrate to those who are reading this report just what is out there for those who go looking for bargains. I needed a gift for a friend, so I went to this web site – and found several coupon codes for FragranceNet.com. I decided to use the following codes, and I planned to try and stack them.

- LSJ30 - $10 off All Orders Over $60

- LSBTS – Free US Shipping On All Orders

I went to the web site, which by the way is one of the best places online to buy both women's and men's fragrances. Discounts of up to 70% off the regular retail price are the norm here, and these are the genuine brands, just like what you find at department stores – no imitations! I noticed that a free gift was available with any purchase – a cute compact mirror. This happens quite a bit on the various retail web sites. So what if it has an advertisement for the web site on it? A freebie is a freebie!

It was no trouble for me to quickly select over $60 worth of products. My choices were-

- Diamonds and Emeralds Gift Set by Elizabeth Taylor - Retail Price $65 – FragranceNet's price $28.79

- Diamonds and Emeralds Shower Gel - Retail Price $27.50 - FragranceNet's price $12.29

- Red Door by Elizabeth Arden Body Powder - Retail Price $24.50 – FragranceNet's price $13.79

- Red Door by Elizabeth Arden Shower Gel - Retail Price $25.00 – FragranceNet's price $14.79

I then went to my online shopping bag. My subtotal was $61.16. I entered the coupon code for free shipping in the box, and clicked the "Apply" button.

Then, I entered the code for $10.00 off all orders over $60. Yes, even though my order was just $1.16 over, I am still eligible to use this code.

My subtotal was now $51.16. I did not have to pay sales tax, as there is no FragranceNet store in the city where I live. So, I got a retail value of $142.00 worth of perfume and bath items for $51.16!

My friend is going to think I am very generous. Everyone who buys perfume knows how much it costs at regular prices, yet no one has to know that you are a smart shopper and are able to buy it at such a great discount... unless you want to let them in on your secret!

See how much fun it is to shop online with coupon codes?

I think just a little more research is necessary for you, dear reader, to see how simple this is and how much money you can save. Besides – a little retail therapy never hurt anyone!

Go back to currentcodes.com to select another code. My next web stop is a site you have probably heard of called Amazon.com. Amazon is a wonderful place to shop online, as they have a little of everything for sale – even food!

How to Increase Sales through Discounted Coupon Codes

There is a Kellogg's promotion going on where you buy $49 or more of Kellogg's, Keebler, Cheez-It, Carrs, Famous Amos, and Worthington Loma Linda products, and get $20 off and free shipping with the coupon code KELLOGG1.

This is an excellent deal – have you noticed the price of one box of cereal at the grocery store lately? Smart coupon shoppers have known for years that you should stock up when the price is right – and when you have a good coupon!

Here are my selections:

- Kellogg's Pop-Tarts Frosted Hot Fudge Sundae - 14.7 ounce box, each containing 8 Pop-Tarts – Case of 12 boxes - $23.55- This is a super, super price even without the additional savings of the coupon code – less than $2.00 a box!

- Kellogg's Favorite Assortment - 96 Single-Serving Bowls of 7 different cereals – Cocoa Krispies, Raisin Bran, Apple Jacks, Froot Loops, Frosted Flakes, Corn Pops, and Frosted Mini Wheats - $39.17 - Another super price even without the coupon code! Cereal @ .35 cents a bowl with no waste!

Subtotal of this order is $62.72. After the $20 coupon code was applied, my total is $42.72 with free shipping and no sales tax. That's a lot of food for the money!

My next stop is to check out a coupon code that appeared in an email from daleandthomaspopcorn.com. This is absolutely the best popcorn, and one of Oprah's "Favorite Things". The coupon code I received is NANNY7 for $20 off of any purchase.

A quick scan of the web site shows a six-pack popcorn variety pack which contains six foot long bags of assorted flavors of gourmet

Anne Marie Collins

popcorn for $28.00. After the coupon code was applied, the price came down to $8.00. Shipping was $7.95… no code for free shipping this time, darn it! $15.95 for this quantity of gourmet popcorn is still an excellent deal, though!

My last stop was at Macys.com, where I found a beautiful Jones New York Sweater with a retail price of $159.99, sale price $29.99. Shipping was 99 cents with the coupon code 99CENTS. This will be another great gift for a family member.

Isn't it amazing how much you can save shopping online with coupon codes?

Chapter 8 - Reasons for Using Coupon Codes

Have you ever trudged through the mall, going into store after store looking for just the right birthday gift for your best friend? Or, have you ever tried to find an article of clothing in a particular color shade, only to be told over and over, "Sorry, we don't have that in stock."? How about a popular book, DVD movie or music CD that you just have to have, but to your dismay, every store you check has sold out of the title?

Maybe you are buying a wedding gift for your cousin. She wants a certain silverware pattern, and so far you've had no luck in finding it. In desperation, you haul out the Yellow Pages and call each store listed that you think might have the elusive pattern, but again, you are out of luck. Or maybe your favorite curling iron or electric razor has stopped working . You go back to the store where you purchased it, only to find that they no longer sell that particular brand.

Were you one of the many people who were standing in line this past holiday season outside of an electronics superstore at the crack of dawn, after camping out on the sidewalk all night? You were hoping and praying that when the doors opened, you would be one of the select few who were able to purchase one of the latest and greatest video game systems that the store had received a shipment of only 10 units the day before.

Perhaps you and a group of your friends gathered outside the Ticketmaster box office early in the evening and stood in line until they opened at midnight in order to grab concert tickets for your favorite music act before they were all sold out.

Or, maybe you need airline tickets, but you only want to spend a certain amount. You know you are supposed to be able to get a good deal if you purchase your tickets two weeks in advance, but when you call the airlines, they quote you an outrageous price that's nothing like the price you expected to pay.

In all of these scenarios, shopping online with a valid coupon code could save you time, trouble, and money. You could spend a pleasant hour browsing stores on the web for a gift that would thrill your best friend, and if you used a coupon code when paying for it, you could either pocket the difference, or maybe put it toward a little bit nicer gift than you had originally planned to give.

That shirt you are looking for in just the right shade of red can be easily found on the Internet. There are hundreds of clothing web sites. Most have photos of the items they sell, color charts, and size charts. Some even have virtual models that you can customize with

How to Increase Sales through Discounted Coupon Codes

your own measurements, then use to "try on" the clothes. You would more than likely have no trouble at all finding exactly what you are looking for, pay a bargain price with the help of a coupon code, and enjoy the process to boot.

Popular DVDs and music CDs and best-seller books can sell out online as well as in a brick and mortar store. But, many places online that sell these items will allow you to preorder them well before the date they are due to be released. The price is almost always better in an online store. Why? Because of the coupon code that is generally issued in anticipation of the rush of people who want to preorder. You get an excellent price, and sometimes free shipping when the item is sent to you.

Items that seem almost impossible to find or that may have been discontinued are often quite easy to find on the web. It's much easier to use a search engine to track down that elusive silverware pattern than it is to go from store to store or spend half the day on the phone looking for it.

There are retail web sites specializing in china and silverware which have hundreds and hundreds of patterns for you to choose from. Most of these stores offer to do whatever they can to help you locate exactly the pattern you seek. And, you'd be surprised at just how often this type of store offers a coupon code for its customers.

Discontinued or hard to find small electrical appliances such as curling irons and razors can be located on the web by using a special search engine that finds such items easily, often still in the original packaging,

A search on a comparison shopping web site such as BizRate.com or Pricegrabber.com will bring back a list of stores which sell the item you want, plus a list of the prices ranging from low to high.

Anne Marie Collins

Add a coupon code to one of the low prices, and you're all set for several more years with your favorite small appliance that you thought you'd never see again.

As for that concert ticket, or even a movie ticket for the latest box office hit, both can be easily booked online at Ticketmaster.com for concert tickets, and Fandango.com for movie tickets. There are even coupon codes available online for these establishments!

Ticketmaster has had codes available that for example will give you a $98 ticket to a musical for $60, half off on certain movie tickets, and 20% off on Ringling Brothers Circus tickets.

Fandango's codes have ranged from Buy one, get one free to a $1 movie ticket. This is the easiest and best way to go to a concert or movie. No hassle, no stress. Order online, get a discount by using a coupon code, and pick your tickets up at the theater the day or evening of the show. What could be easier?

Online retailers are pretty savvy folks themselves. When you shop online at a web site for the first time, you are usually invited to register. Of course, you can decline, as you can still do business with the merchant even without giving him your email address and other pertinent info, but some information is needed so your order can be tracked, if necessary. Registration does make it easier when you go back to shop with a merchant for the second time. All you need to do is sign in with your email and password, and your information will be placed onto the order form for you.

Drugstore.com is a retailer that takes this a step further. When you buy items from their web site such as health and beauty aids or vitamins, they calculate the time it should take you to use them up. After this time has passed, then send you an email with a gentle

How to Increase Sales through Discounted Coupon Codes

reminder that it's time to order again! Very convenient... and very smart of Drugstore.com!

This is one way a website lures you back for that next purchase. Another way they can get your attention is to send well-timed emails to you that outline any sales they may be having. Usually, a coupon code or two will be included in this email, for you are now considered to be a "preferred customer". These stores want your business!

Online coupon codes can turn up in the most surprising places. You would not think that a high end store would offer much in the way of coupon codes or discounts, but they most certainly do, and good ones, too. This is a fantastic way to own luxury items that you may not be able to afford otherwise. It is not an unusual occurrence to buy a beautiful sweater that retails for hundreds of dollars for just a fraction of that price when you combine a sale with a coupon code.

Another reason why you should use online coupon codes is to be able to take advantage of the vast assortment of goods and services available on the Internet at a bargain price. If you live in a part of the country that does not have certain national chain stores, you can still shop at any of them from the comfort of your home. Or, if you live far from a big city and do not have many stores to choose from when you get ready to shop for clothing, items for your home, or anything else, you can turn to the Internet to find what you are looking for. Combine a world of choices with a coupon code that will save you money, and you have got quite a winning combination!

Chapter 9- Maximizing Coupon Codes

Things to Avoid

Now that you are all excited about the money you can save using coupon codes, there are a few things you need to know in order to keep yourself safe while shopping online.

- A disturbing trend has come to light on auction sites such as EBay where unsuspecting shoppers are actually buying coupon codes that are supposed to be free! This is not a good idea, and steps as being taken as of this writing to have the offending auctions pulled. Why would you want to pay for something that is meant to be free? The people who are running these auctions are

How to Increase Sales through Discounted Coupon Codes

counting on the fact that some shoppers will not realize that these codes are available for free all over the web.

- Stick with stores that you know are legitimate when shopping online with coupon codes. If you run across a web store offering you an incredible coupon code like $75 off when you spend $100, or something equally as absurd, run, don't walk! This web site is more than likely after personal information such as your credit card number, and if you give it out to them, you may find a lot of unauthorized charges on your statement next month. As the old saying goes, if it seems just too good to be true, it probably is.

- When searching for a web site than contains information about online shopping and coupon codes, make sure you are using a site that offers you fresh, up to date codes. It's very discouraging to click through to an expired coupon code thinking you are about to get a good deal, and instead you get nothing. Don't settle for a site that just has a bunch of codes up on a page, either. At the very least, you want links to the online stores where the codes are to be used.

- Choose a coupon code web site that seems friendly. You want to be able to ask questions when you need to, so a web site with a forum where shoppers can congregate and exchange ideas and thoughts about online shopping is ideal, especially for someone new to online shopping. In the event that there is no forum page then look for an email address, where you can at least contact the owner of the web page.

- You should be able to view the coupon codes on a web site without having to give out your email address. Now, don't be alarmed when you come across a site that does ask for this information. You don't have to give it out if you don't want to. But usually, the site asks you to register if you want to take part in the forums, or to receive occasional emails about the web site. If a web site is asking for your information seemingly for no reason, back off. They may be simply harvesting email addresses, and if you give yours out, you may well wind up with an email inbox full of spam.

Get More from Your Coupons

Now that you have read about how easy it is to save some serious money with online coupon codes, it's time to learn a few tips to help you to make the most of the codes you will be using.

- You're ready to check out and use that great coupon code you found for $10 off when you spend $20, but your items total $19.86. Sure, you could add another item that costs a dollar, but why spend more than you have to? There is a very handy little tool that helps you find what online shoppers commonly call "filler items".

- Filler items are things that cost very little, and hence are used to make up those last few cents needed to bring your order total up to a certain amount. It would take you a mighty long time to go through a huge web site like Amazon.com looking for items that cost 10 cents (yes, such items do exist) so Pricetaker's tool is innovative and quite a timesaver, too.

- To use this tool, choose your store from the drop down box, then enter the price range you want to see items from. Try .01 to .05 for starters – you will be surprised how many items come up! Now you can pick out one or more things to bring your order total to the amount needed!

- The web site Couponwinner.com has a nifty little tool called Coupon Scout. It allows you to select a category, choose up to

5 different stores from a long list, then compare the coupon codes they have to offer. It is a quick way to see what's available, especially if you are in a hurry.

- If you want to be a really smart online shopper, and the idea of missing a good deal makes you almost want to cry, choose several of your favorite sites that offer coupon codes. Bookmark them in their own folder so you can refer back to them daily. And, it goes without saying – always search for a valid coupon code before every online purchase!

- Everyone has their favorite "real" stores… those you actually walk into and make a purchase as opposed to buying an item online. One of the best tips I ever received was to always check the online stores for coupon code specials before you shop their brick and mortar counterparts. Often you will find a better deal online than in the actual store, and then you take action and buy the item.

- Plan your shopping so that you are able to meet any purchase requirements necessary to use the online code. If you have to spend $50 in order to use the coupon code, look the web site over carefully and make a list of the things you need and could buy in order to bring your total spent up to the amount you need.

- Choose your favorite online stores. They will offer newsletters or special mailings to their customers who have signed up to receive them, and often these will have coupon codes in the form of special discount links that the general public does not see.

- Coupon code web sites will also publish newsletters, and it would be worth your while to subscribe to a few of them as well to keep abreast of any new codes that have been released. These stores and/or web sites won't fill up your inbox, nor will they spam you!

- Generally, you can expect an email from an online store or web site maybe once a week – usually less often – but sometimes, more often. It all depends on how many new coupon codes there are.

- Think of it like this... receiving emails from your favorite online stores can actually save you a lot of time. You won't have to go to the actual website in order to keep up with the latest deals.

- Read. Read magazines. Read newspapers. And, watch commercials! The idea here is to keep up with the latest trends. You need to know how much things cost in order to be able to determine whether or not something is a good buy.

- Paying attention to prices can actually save you money in the long run. A coupon code is not a good deal if you use it to buy something that is a cheap imitation of a quality product.

- Don't snatch up the first bargain you see for a really big ticket item, coupon code or not. Make certain you can't get it for a better price anywhere else. You never know when an even better bargain may be lurking just around the corner!

- Try not to be in a hurry when you shop. This is yet another reason why shopping online is so great! Think about it – Don't you think the stress level is a lot lower for someone who is sitting at home, relaxed at their computer with their feet propped up, surfing the Internet for bargains than it is for the person standing in a store inside a crowded mall trying to catch the eye of a salesperson in order to ask a question?.

How to Increase Sales through Discounted Coupon Codes

- Would you like to make money for your child's college education while you are shopping? There are web sites that will give you back a small percentage of the money you use to purchase items. One of them is called Upromise. Once you sign up for Upromise, you can go through their web site to get to retailer's web sites. When you buy something, a percentage of what you spend is deposited into your account. It is a painless way to save a little money which can build up over time into a surprisingly large amount!

Chapter 10- Where Can Your Customers Find Your Coupons?

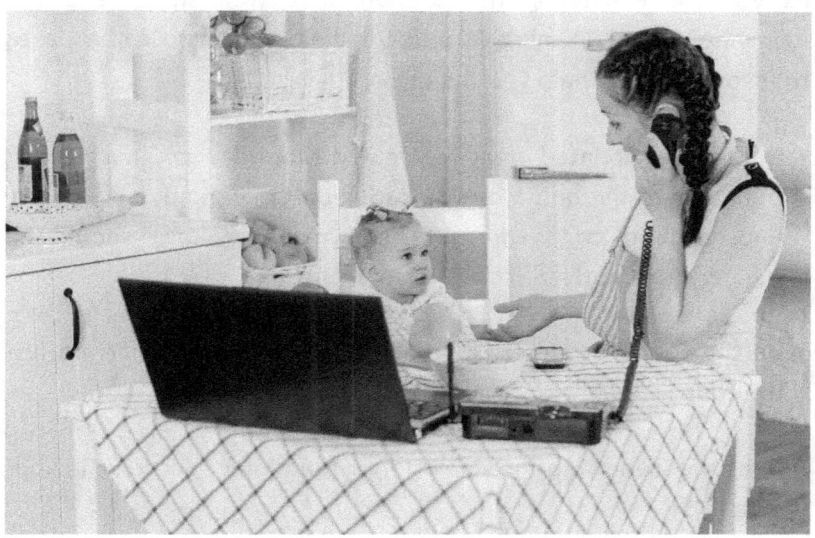

Web sites that list current online coupons abound. A Google search will reveal a surprising number of pages dedicated to supplying you with these codes. Some search terms to use when looking for coupon codes include –

- Online coupons

- Coupon codes

- Promotional codes

- Shopping codes

- Discount codes

If you want to save as much money as possible, taking the time to review each coupon website would be a good idea, as this is the

How to Increase Sales through Discounted Coupon Codes

best way to see what they have to offer. Then, you can choose a few favorites to come back and check each day.

As you are evaluating the coupon code web sites, keep the following criteria in mind in order to help you choose the pages that you think will help you the most.

- Is the site updated daily? Weekly? Monthly? Or, not at all? Updates are the only way you can keep up with any new codes. And, expired codes do not help anyone. These should be removed promptly.

- Do the coupon codes include all of the offer details, or are just the code listed?

- Does the web site offer a newsletter that you can receive in your email?

- How easy is it to find codes on the web site?

- Does the web site offer codes for most of the online retailers I do business with?

Why would you want to check a coupon web site on a daily basis if you aren't planning on shopping every day? Well, you might be surprised that you will save the most money if you do not limit yourself to only using a coupon code when you need to buy something.

Often, coupon codes that offer excellent savings will pop up on these sites, and are so popular that after a day, they are pulled by the company. Whether the retailer has begun to lose money because of so many shoppers taking advantage of a good deal is a question that has remained unanswered.

Don't just scan the main pages of a coupon web site! You'll find that often, the true gold in the site is in its forum. The discussions that take place in coupon shopping forums can be fascinating. You get to read about the code deals that other people have found, which may well be the perfect deal for you, too.

You can also learn about any problem codes that have expired or do not work correctly for one reason or another. The forums also give shoppers an outlet where they can discuss any online stores that are especially worth shopping in, or that they have had some sort of problem with. This can alert you to retailers that you might want to add to your list of favorites, or that you may want to avoid.

There is power in numbers, and you might be surprised at what a group of shoppers can accomplish when they all band together. A forum member might have a problem with an online store and not know exactly what to do. Other members come to her aid with helpful advice, and the problem is generally rectified quickly.

One of the main points to remember is that with online coupon codes, as with many other ways to save money, "When you snooze, you lose". Don't miss out - grab a good deal while you can, and either stockpile your purchases so that you can settle back for a few months without having to purchase these items again at full price, put them away for gifts later in the year, or share your bounty with someone who is less fortunate.

Some Popular Coupon Code Websites

Experience is often the best teacher when it comes to getting the most out of online shopping and coupon codes. The following listing of coupon code web sites is made up of the ones that I use most frequently for information regarding online shopping, and for valid coupon codes. They make the fascinating hobby of bargain

How to Increase Sales through Discounted Coupon Codes

shopping even more fun! Your mileage may vary, but do check these sites out to help you learn and save!

- FreelanceByU – Save Money without Compromising Your Lifestyle.

This is without a doubt my favorite site. Angela Hresan, the site's owner, has been featured on The Today Show for her knowledge and status as an expert on living lavishly for less. Her motto is "Never pay full price for anything, ever!"

The web site is packed with information that may be a little bit overwhelming at first. Just dig in and start reading, and watch your savings began to mount up quickly!

- There are articles that explain all about online coupons and how to get the most for your money when shopping online,

- A large listing of current coupon codes,

- A freebies page,

- A sweepstakes page,

- A very active forum.

The forum is the heart and soul of the web site. So much goes on in the forum that it is almost as if it is a little city within itself! Here are just a few of the topics that are covered in the Freelancebyu forum –

- Good Deal Alerts

These deals and offers are extremely helpful because the end date of each is listed... a pertinent fact that isn't always in this kind of listing.

- Free Magazines

Yes, believe it or not, you can get free subscriptions to many popular magazines with NO CATCH! I'm sure this is good advertising for the companies, and they just write it off.

- Help in Finding Deals

If you are looking for a coupon code on something in particular and are having trouble finding it, let the Freelancebyu experts help you look!

- Rebates and Refunds

This is another money saving hobby that blends in quite well with online shopping and coupon codes.

- Maken Baken

This is a place where money making strategies, including, but not limited to, online shopping and coupon codes are discussed.

- The Box Man Cometh

A fun subject! This is where shoppers can share what the "Box Man", for example, the UPS or FedEx delivery person brought to them today.

How to Increase Sales through Discounted Coupon Codes
- Expired Offers

Extremely helpful when you can't remember the details of that great offer you did! These archives are cleared out periodically to make room for more. Yes, there are that many coupon codes and online shopping deals!

Angie also has a newsletter that goes out whenever there is an especially good online shopping deal. This can be a couple of times a day, or every few days… it just depends on what is going on in the online shopping world.

Trust me when I say that this newsletter and web site are well worth your time if you are interested in saving money with coupon codes and online shopping!

Another great web site that is quite popular the Dealtaker. It's a Sister site to Pricetaker.com, which was discussed above. Dealtaker.com is a very well organized and through web site that lists coupon codes and information for/from over 1400 stores! Some of the other neat things on this web site that will compliment your online coupon code shopping are –

- Gift Taker.com This is a neat way to let family and friends know about items that you run across on your online shopping expeditions that you would like to have for yourself. It can be your very own online wish list, and unlike the wish lists that are store-specific like the one at Amazon.com, you can place items from any online store onto your personal list. Use it for birthdays, Christmas, weddings, baby showers, or any other gift-giving occasion.

- DealTaker has a web page that features a huge selection of gift cards/gift certificates available for purchase. Gift cards make excellent gifts when you don't know what to buy for someone, and it's really convenient to have them all on one page like this. When you click on the link below the image of each gift card, it takes you directly to the web page where you can purchase the gift card.

- DealTaker also has a forum which lists freebies from all over the web, a forum where shoppers can discuss online coupon code deals they have found, and the gem of the site, the stores page. This is where all of the coupon codes are listed, and boy, is it an extensive list! When you click on a store name, it takes you to a page where each code is showcased in a graphic that looks like a paper coupon... you know, the kind you used to use before you discovered online coupons! It's a very cute way of displaying the codes, and makes them easy to read, too.

A cute web site that goes by the name of A Full Cup has not only a very active forum full of friendly shoppers, but several coupon generators that allow you to print coupons from the web to take to the store with you. You can print coupons from Target, Food Lion, and an ever-changing variety of miscellaneous stores.

Most online shoppers are familiar with Fat Wallet. It has a category for every type of online coupon you can imagine, a price comparison page, and a forum where you can ask any sort of question about online shopping and get a quick answer. An ongoing thread in the Fat Wallet forum is a listing of hard to find telephone numbers for those times when you need to call a retailer about a problem in their store, or with an online order from their store. This information can be hard to locate, and it is very nice to have it all together in one spot.

The web page of CurrentCodes is not a very fancy page, but the information contained on it is priceless! CurrentCodes lists codes

How to Increase Sales through Discounted Coupon Codes

ONLY... no deals or online sales. They feel they can better serve the internet population by focusing solely on the codes. There is a space that lists the newest codes that have come in, and another section where you can browse for coupon codes by merchant, alphabetically, or by category.

DealHunting.com is another huge database of coupon codes. This web site will alert you when a great deal becomes available if you sign up with your email address. They seem to have codes for a lot of online stores that the other coupon code websites do not list... specialty stores such as

- Bits and Pieces, a jigsaw puzzle/game store

- Harry and David, who sells fruit and gourmet chocolates

- San Francisco Music Box Company, which features music boxes and other collectibles

- Hallmark, of greeting card, keepsake ornament, and gift fame

- Design Toscano, a neat store with unique gifts and home and garden décor

DealHunting also is one of the few coupon code websites that lists Canadian offers. The web site offers an active message board/forum where lively shopping discussions are always taking place.

Centsible.net not only lists coupon codes for online shopping, but also has links to the websites of a huge list of both American and Canadian grocery store chains. This is extremely useful! You can now check out your favorite grocery store's online flyer before you go food shopping and in most cases, print out a list of items to buy.

Anne Marie Collins

Seeing the advertised specials online is a novelty that you won't soon tire of, and it is quite a timesaver.

The web site of RetailMeNot is a slick-looking site, kind of retro in design with video tutorials on how to use coupon codes online to save money. RetailMeNot also has an innovative little device called a Quick Access Bookmarklet. To use it, you first place a link into your Favorites in your browser. Then, whenever you are at a retailer's web site doing some shopping, and want to know if there are any coupon codes available for that site, you just click on the Bookmarklet. If there are any online codes, another window will pop up containing the codes. What a neat little thing to have!

RetailMeNot also sends out a weekly newsletter to those who have signed up to receive it. They have just recently begun to offer a forum for discussion of all things coupon.

Coupon Mountain offers coupon codes that are updated several different times a day from over 2000 stores in categories such as

- Arts and Collectibles

- Automotive

- Baby and Maternity

- Books

- Cell Phones

- Clothing and Accessories

- Computers

How to Increase Sales through Discounted Coupon Codes

- Dating and Personals (dating and personal coupon codes? Wow!)

- Electronics

- Finance

- Flowers, Gifts, and Gourmet

- Food and Beverage

- Freebies

- Groceries

- Health and Beauty

- Home and Garden

- Internet Services

- Jewelry and Watches

- Movies

- Music

- Office Products

- Pet Supplies

- Photography

- Sporting Goods

- Toys

- Travel

- Video Games

Coupon Cabin is a web site that has been featured in several media outlets such as —

- The Chicago Tribune

- The Wall Street Journal

- ABC Television Network

- NBC Television Network

- CBS Television Network

- Fox Television Network

- Fox news Network

- USA Today

- Good Morning America

- Consumer Reports Money

There is a long listing of all of the different cities where the television programs that featured Coupon Cabin were shown, and an equally long listing of all of the local papers in the United States where stories about Coupon Cabin were featured. Also listed are quite a few radio stations where Coupon Cabin has been given exposure, and finally, a list of print magazines and online publications where Coupon Cabin has been featured. This is very impressive! As of this writing, there were 3233 active and valid

How to Increase Sales through Discounted Coupon Codes

coupons and deals on this web site. An animated demo, with sound, is provided so that you can see how to best use the web site.

Coupon Cabin also has a sister site called CheapUncle, which is a deal finder. When you type in the name of a product, the database is searched, and the best priced deals are listed for you to choose from. This can save you time and allow you to compare prices more efficiently.

Slick Deals is a coupon code website that has a very good feature for shoppers who want to stay on top of things. It is called Deal Alert. Once you have registered on the site, you can set up your forum account to email you when any keyword that you specify - such as camera, sweater, and laptop... whatever product you are interested in receiving updated deal information on – appears in the forum with a new coupon code or deal. Slick Deals has a very active forum, filled with shoppers who are always on the lookout for bargains, so the chances of you being among the first to know about the latest great deal are very good!

Reesycakes.com is a shopping web site with a rather interesting name. It bills itself as a "shopping companion" with a detailed listing of stores, with reviews to come, a nice listing of coupon codes, sales and events, and other special features you are sure to enjoy.

You'll smile when you see this web page. Naughtycodes may make you think you've clicked somewhere you shouldn't have. In reality though, it is a pretty good little web site with a long list of online stores and coupon codes.

A web site called 1001 Coupons at claims to be the largest listing of codes on the Internet, and they do indeed seem to have coupon codes for places such as Walgreens.com, The Vitamin Shoppe.com, and Food Network.com, retailers that are a bit harder to locate valid coupon codes for. 1001 Coupons will send you "the best" coupon codes every week in your email if you sign up with them.

When you visit ultimatecoupons, you will see that they seem to offer a little bit of everything!

- Message Boards

- A directory of retailers all over the web with clearance and closeout prices

- Product Reviews – a helpful listing of sites all over the Internet that give opinions on a wide range of products. This can be very helpful when trying to decide between two or more brands.

- A section that enables you to find coupons local to your area for such things as restaurants, movies, etc.

- A listing of manufacturer's coupons that you can print on your computer, have mailed to your home, or emailed to you free of charge.

- A freebie page

- A coupon blog

- Deals of the Day

- Cash Back Shopping

- Buying Guides – my favorite part of the site. This lists several links, including Consumer Reports Online, where shoppers can go

How to Increase Sales through Discounted Coupon Codes

to learn more about an item they are considering the purchase of.

- A Web Shopping Guide that really has a lot of useful tips about online shopping in general.

- Finally, Ultimate Coupons.com offers one of the best coupon and deals newsletters around. Be sure to sign up for this one so you can stay informed on all of the latest coupon codes!

CouponCode.com is a smaller web site than some of the others, listing only around 500 coupon codes at any one time. But, the codes are valid ones, and the web site itself is well laid out and easy to use. The site is working hard in order to update and expand, and has been mentioned on NBC Television, ABC Television, and in US News and World Report magazine. There is a listing of Popular Coupons here, those which many people have used. Looking this list over is a good way to see what some of the best coupon codes are.

Sometimes it seems like all of these coupon code web sites were named by the same person! Since the names of some of them sound alike, it would be easy to get them confused if they all did not have such different options for smart shoppers. The web site at couponshack is no exception. This web site used to be called Coupon Monkey, so I guess with the name change came a new look as well.

Bright graphics and a crisp, clean template make this web site a powerful ally in determining which coupon codes are best. Coupon Shack offers Exclusive Coupons, which were created especially for this web site by the stores you see listed. They also have a very good list of the most popular coupon codes, a special Travel category which is extremely useful if you need to purchase a last minute airline ticket, and a financial category which does an excellent job of explaining such things as mortgages, loans, credit cards, and insurance.

Online shopping has become more popular than ever before. It is estimated that 78 percent of Internet users are now shopping online. That's an awful lot of people who have discovered how much easier it is to click their mouse than to fight the crowds. Everyone loves to get a good deal, and the word has spread that the deals are all over the Internet!

Now that you have read this report, you are armed with quite a bit of valuable information, and the tools that you need to become a super shopper! You will regularly save money with each and every purchase you make with an online coupon code. These codes are one of the best-kept secrets of the Internet, and allow you to find bargains that your family and friends won't believe. With just a little patience and time, there is virtually nothing that you cannot find on the Internet at a lower price than what you would pay at a regular store.

So settle back, grab a cup of coffee, and... Let's go shopping!

ABOUT THE AUTHOR

Anne Marie Collins is a housewife and mother to five beautiful children. The family owns a laundry business, which she manages as her husband works at a bank.

Anne has a very busy schedule that's why she does what she needs to do in the most efficient manner to avoid repetition of tasks. This goes the same for her business. Once she creates a marketing strategy, she studies every detail first before it is implemented. As a matter of fact, it is her careful planning and great attention to detail that made her business flourish.

Anne holds a degree in Communications.

www.ingramcontent.com/pod-product-compliance
Lightning Source LLC
Chambersburg PA
CBHW070824220526
45466CB00002B/750